Real Mothers

A Bible study about mothers for mothers

Joyce Long

CrossLink Publishing
Rapid City, SD
www.crosslink.org

CrossLink Publishing
www.crosslink.org

ISBN 978-0-9816983-4-2

For My Mother

Dedicated to Eva Nell [Fortner] Hasler, whose
steadfast faithfulness and servant's heart has blessed
many lives during her 84 years. Thanks Mom, for
all you that do and all that you are!

Proverbs 31:10-31

Table of Contents

Introduction

Real Mothers is unique in that it studies everyday problems encountered in the lives of eight mothers of the Bible: Eve, Sarah, Rebekah, Jochebed, Hannah, Elizabeth, Mary, and the mother of James and John, Salome. This isn't just an academic exercise to read and fill in the blank. It's designed to be very practical with each lesson structured into five sections thematically organized by the word *time*, which is a precious commodity and too often nonexistent for busy moms.

Real Time is simply a quick introduction telling a brief story that relates to today's mothers. The Bible study section, ***Word Time***, is designed for the ladies to do together for approximately 30 minutes. ***Life Time*** asks practical questions that interweave the biblical example with today's concerns, generating discussion usually lasting 20 minutes. The two final sections, ***Own Time*** and ***Next Time***, are designed as optional homework. ***Own Time*** features reflective questions designed for personal prayer and application while ***Next Time*** briefly previews next week's lesson.

Real Mothers is a solution to a need for reaching young mothers with no extra time for homework and minimal biblical background. It was first taught on Sunday morning during the church's adult education hour. It was later revised for an outreach Bible study held at a local mobile home community. An inner-city Indianapolis mission has used this study as part of their outreach to their preschool's mothers. Nationally, this study would benefit any Mothers of Preschoolers (MOPS) group.

Because this study has been taught, transformation has happened in the lives of several of the women. God's Word is powerful in showing us how to be real—not perfect, but real. God can use his Word and the study of these intriguing biblical mothers to change women in ways that will touch lives for generations.

Real Mothers: *A Bible study about mothers for mothers*

1. **Real Parenting** – Because God is a parent, our heavenly Father, he understands all the heartaches, headaches, and delight of real parenting. An overview of God's example sets the stage for this Bible study. The scriptural focus is **Isaiah 66:7-13** and **1 Thessalonians 2:6-12.**

2. **Eve** – As our parent, God also created us through Adam and Eve. This lesson examines the first example of disobedience through both God's and Eve's eyes. Original sin is presented very simply in the context of obedience versus disobedience. Eve's sons, Cain and Abel, are also studied in this same context.

3. **Sarah** – Originally named Sarai, this beautiful but aging woman struggled with impatience. Mothers often struggle with this same kind of doubt, worry, and impatience that Sarah felt wondering how God would fulfill his promise. How faith and works are integrated into parenting make this lesson very practical.

4. **Rebekah** – Her independence was both her strength and weakness, especially when she alone decided that Jacob needed his father's birthright. When the father favors one child and the mother another, things can get pretty messy. It happened in Rebekah's family, and it often happens today in families.

5. **Jochebed** – Life's difficult circumstances often result in difficult choices. Jochebed had to choose whether to keep her son, fearing for his life, or to let him go, hoping for his future. Her love for him prevailed as she gave him up for adoption.

6. **Hannah** – For women who have struggled with becoming pregnant or staying pregnant, Hannah's story resonates. Another mother, who just happened to be her husband's other wife, compounded this young woman's despair. Her emotional upheaval bewildered her husband, who interpreted her distress to mean that she wasn't satisfied with their relationship.

7. **Elizabeth** – Each of us needs an encourager in our lives. An unwed, pregnant younger woman, the mother of Jesus Christ needed her cousin Elizabeth to help her through the physical, emotional, and spiritual aspects of her pregnancy. As a true friend and mentor, Elizabeth encouraged her, blessing both Mary and the baby she carried.

8. **Mary** – No other mother in history has been as revered and worshiped as the mother of our Lord Jesus Christ. Mary's acceptance of Gabriel's news and her willingness to believe, trust, and rejoice in God's will for her life caused her to be *highly favored*. Women everywhere could learn from her righteous example.

9. **Salome** – If ever there were a contemporary, soccer-mom-type mother in the Bible, the mother of James and John fills those shoes. Of all of the mothers profiled in this study, Salome seemed to be the most involved in her sons' lives, even as they became young adults.

Real Love – A brief summary of these mothers of the Bible, this chapter's focus is very practical. Participants will evaluate their own family circumstances, pray for their children, and write a description of the legacy of faith they want their children and/or grandchildren to have.

Lesson 1 – *Real Parenting*

Real Time

No mother ever forgets the details of giving birth. We may forget our child's name on occasion or, on a really hectic day, where our children are, but rarely will any of us ever hesitate to give an exact play-by-play account of our children's birth. At formal dinner parties, wedding receptions, and especially baby showers, we form a special bond by comparing notes about how long labor took, how our husbands responded, and how we felt when seeing our baby for the first time. But giving birth doesn't necessarily equate to being a parent. Parenting can be a lot more painful.

The pain I most often experience is not knowing how much to do for or how to relate to my children. This dilemma really began in the hospital hours after our son was born. The nurse came in and noticed that we had the disposable diaper on backwards. It just seemed to make sense to pull the tape to the back. Before we could correct our first parenting mistake, he was taken away for his first photo shoot—dirty diaper and all. It seems we've been just a step behind ever since. Fast forward two decades, and we're still not sure what his favorite home cooked meal is. It seems he went from craving corn dogs to spicy Thai food in one quantum leap. Playing catch-up as a mother has always been stressful.

So I began to wonder how mothers of the Bible handled their stress. I wanted to discover how they related to their children, what their family responsibilities were, and how their husbands helped them. What I found is that after the Garden of Eden, family life was far from perfect. Mothers weren't perfect. Kids weren't perfect. Children fought, even killed, and were constantly jealous of each other. Fathers were sometimes clueless, sometimes even speechless, and often too busy. Does any of this sound familiar?

But not so surprisingly, God took ordinary women like you and me and answered their prayers, calmed their fears, and as the apostle Paul stated so well in **Romans 8:28,** "worked in all things for the good of those who love him, who have been called according to his purpose." God's purpose for us as mothers is to love him and teach our children to love him. Together let's discover how mothers in the Bible passionately loved God, how he worked all things, even bad things, for their ultimate good.

We'll look at the Bible's own First Lady – Eve – and wonder why a bite of fruit was worth forfeiting free rent in paradise. Then we'll move on to Sarah and laugh with her as she realized she was pregnant at 90. (I'm fairly certain that I wouldn't be laughing.) With Rebekah, we'll see the effects of sibling rivalry and parental favoritism. With Jochebed, we'll learn that faith often means risking a loss of control. Then we'll cry with Hannah as she struggles with infertility and another woman's meanness.

In the New Testament, we'll see how cousins Elizabeth and Mary encourage each other and then share extraordinary birthing experiences of extraordinary sons. Finally we'll end with Salome, the mother of James and John, whom I affectionately call the Kool-Aid Mom of the Bible.

What I pray that we learn from studying these fascinating mothers is that although they weren't perfect and neither were their circumstances, they served not only their own families, but they loved and served God. In their faithfulness, they survived and even flourished in their far-from-perfect circumstances, providing a real legacy for both their own children and generations to come.

Word Time

One of the reasons I enjoy the book of Isaiah in the Old Testament is that God's heart for his people is so vividly revealed. **Isaiah 66:7-13** compares delivering and nursing a baby to how God cares for his people. Please read the above passage and answer the following questions:

1. After reading this passage, what do you learn about giving birth?

2. From these verses, what do you learn about a mother's care for her newborn?

3. Compare how God's love and a new mother's love are the same.

4. In **Psalm 139:13-16**, David writes about how intimately God created us. What insight do you find in this passage about how well God knows us?

Because our God knows us so well, he models what it means to be a good parent. That's probably why he likes to be called our father. In encouraging the disciples at Thessalonica, Paul talks about how good parents interact with their children. Please read **1 Thessalonians 2:6-12.**

5. In **verse 7**, what word does Paul use to describe how a mother cares for her children?

6. According to **verse 11**, name three ways a father should deal with his children.

    a. _____ them

    b. _____ them

    c. _____ them to

    _____lives worthy of _____.

In the following passages, God's Word talks about honoring our mothers and fathers. Note any blessings and/or promises that come from these precepts or any negative consequences that come from ignoring them. Also note who is speaking in each of these.

	Scripture	Speaker	Promise/ Blessing	Negative Consequence
7.	Deuteronomy 5:16			
8.	Deuteronomy 27:16			
9.	Matthew 15: 3 - 7			
10	Matthew 19:16 - 19			
11	Mark 7: 9 - 13			
12	Mark 10: 18 - 19			
13	Luke 18: 18 – 21			
14	Ephesians 6:2			

It's easy to honor lovable, kind, and fair parents, but it's not always easy to honor those parents who haven't been what God called them to be. Nevertheless, God wants us to honor and love our parents just as he loves us even when we aren't worthy or so lovable ourselves.

In fact, he believes so much in the importance of family that he left heaven to be part of one. Jesus didn't have to come into this world as a baby, submissive to his parents, Mary and Joseph. But the Lord of heaven and earth desired his experience to be as we live—as a baby, as a child, as a teen, and finally as an adult. God loves the family, because he has experienced each phase of what a family is. Now he asks all of us to join his family— as sons and daughters to share an eternal inheritance. "I will be a Father to you, and you will be my sons and daughters," says the Lord Almighty (2 Corinthians 6:18).

Life Time

15. As a mother, what specific things do you do to follow the pattern found in **1 Thessalonians 2:7?**

16. Give yourself a rating 1- 10 with 10 being the highest and explain why you chose that. Be sure to include all the positives that you do as a mother.

    My ranking is _____ because of the following things I do well as a mother:

17. Here are a few things I could improve upon as a mother:

18. Now write out a prayer where you ask the Lord to help you make those changes. Remember what Gabriel told Mary in **Luke 1:37**, "For nothing is impossible with God."

19. Give examples of how you honor your mother and father. How could you improve upon this?

20. Read **Proverbs 23:22**. What good advice is given in this verse?

The following came from a forwarded email message but speaks strongly about how we too often view our mothers as we grow up.

Ages & Stages of Motherhood

- 4 YEARS OF AGE ~ My Mommy can do anything!
- 8 YEARS OF AGE ~ My Mom knows a lot! A whole lot!
- 12 YEARS OF AGE ~ My Mother doesn't really know quite everything.
- 14 YEARS OF AGE ~ Naturally, Mother doesn't know that, either.
- 16 YEARS OF AGE ~ Mother? She's hopelessly old-fashioned.
- 18 YEARS OF AGE ~ That old woman? She's way out-of-date!
- 25 YEARS OF AGE ~ Well, she might know a little bit about it.
- 35 YEARS OF AGE ~ Before we decide, let's get Mom's opinion.
- 45 YEARS OF AGE ~ Wonder what Mom would have thought about it?
- 65 YEARS OF AGE ~ Wish I could talk it over with Mom.

Own Time

This brings to mind what the writer of Hebrews says about maturity.   Read **Hebrews 5:11-14.** Praise him that we don't have to stay milk-fed from the bottle, but we can grow on solid food and apply the wisdom that we've gained from our parents and/or parental figures in our life.

21. Think about any practical wisdom that you learned from your mother or mother figure, and write what comes to mind below:

22. Now write out a prayer of thanksgiving for all that you have been have given—by your heavenly father, by your parents, and/or by both.

Next Time – Eve

Let's meet the first couple by reading **Genesis 2:18-25.** Adam certainly got a surprise when he woke up.

23. Explain why Eve was created.

24. Explain how Eve was created.

25. What was Adam's response to meeting Eve? How does that define their relationship?

Lesson 2 – *Eve*

Real Time

One of the most important things that I've tried to teach my son, aside from loving God and his Word, is that girls love flowers. It's a concept that he doesn't quite grasp mainly because he doesn't yet have a girlfriend. His father has grown in this understanding throughout thirty years of marriage. In our first years of marriage, I would have coveted a bouquet of something once in awhile rather than a small household appliance. His logical thinking would have him reason otherwise.

Now that we are well supplied with gadgets, he's trying to figure out why his bride suddenly wants a new electric can opener for Christmas. A few years back, he would have been scolded for such a tasteless gift. Now due to the old handheld one's rust and my arthritis, a new electric can opener is truly a gift I enjoy. It's no wonder the Adams in our lives are confused by us Eves. They simply can't keep up with our needs and passions—be it a bouquet or a *Sunbeam something*.

But if the truth is known, most women covet anything involving flowers. I'm convinced that one of the reasons my mother was passionate in collecting fine china is that it had flowers on it. Her wedding-gift bone china is delicately inscribed with crimson roses vined throughout its cream background. My love for roses probably began with our eating many a big Thanksgiving meal on those rose-covered plates. Food and flowers—not a bad combination! That divine combination was one God created for Adam and Eve in the Garden of Eden.

For a moment, imagine with me what the Garden of Eden must have been like—walking side by side with the Lord of all creation in the fragrance of the lilies of the valley, stopping together once in awhile to enjoy a fresh bite from an orange tree. Adam and Eve enjoyed a personal relationship with God that we long for and plan on having when his dwelling place again is with mankind **(Revelation 21:3-4).**

In my journalistic interview fantasies, I've always wanted to ask Eve, "What were you thinking? Meals you didn't have to plan or prepare. Surrounded by tropical paradise with the deepest of purple orchids. No shopping for jeans, after-Christmas clearance left-overs, and never ever having to try on a swimsuit." Sounds like paradise to me! And yet Eve wasn't satisfied.

But let's not be too hard on Eve. How is it in our lives that knowing God isn't enough or that our material blessings don't satisfy? No matter what we think, we are not too far removed from Eve, whose Hebrew name "Chavvah" means "living" and "life". Let's get back to the garden and enjoy the fragrance, fellowship, and contentment of simply walking with our Lord because that is his delight.

"The Lord delights in the way of the man whose steps he has made firm; though he stumble, he will not fall, for the Lord upholds him with his hand" (Psalm 37:23-24).

Word Time

1. Please read **Genesis 1:27.** How did God pattern
    man?

2. In **Genesis 2,** God gives us more details about
    the creation of Adam and Eve. Let's focus on
    verses 4-7 and **15-25.**

    How did God form man? Note that some
    scholars believe that the Hebrew word for *man*
    (adam) sounds like and may be related to the
    Hebrew word for *ground* (adamah).

3. Look at **verse 15.** What work did God give
    Adam to do?

4. Focus on **verses 18-20**. What did Adam need that caused God to create woman?

5. **Genesis 2:24** is repeated four other times in the Bible. Note the context of these cross-references and who was quoting the Genesis passage.

    • **Matthew 19:4-6**   • **1 Corinthians 6:16**

    • **Mark 10:6-9**   • **Ephesians 5:28-33**

6. Review **Genesis 2:15-17**. From what tree did God tell them not to eat?

7. What would be the consequences if they ate from that tree?

8. How does the above commandment, first stated in **Genesis 2:17,** relate to parents who desire protection for their children?

9. Do you think Adam and Eve understood what *"you shall surely die"* meant? Please explain.

10. Read **Genesis 3:1-7.** How was Eve deceived by the serpent?

11. Review **verses 4** and **5** in **Genesis 3**. Which of these serpent responses was a lie?

12. Focus on **verse 6**. What three attributes of the fruit appealed to Eve?

    a).

    b).

    c).

13. In the New Testament, find **1 John 2:16** where worldly sin is described. Write down its three attributes below:

    a).

    b)

    c).

14. Do you see a relationship between **1 John 2:16** and **Genesis 3:6**? If so, explain what that is.

15. Read **Genesis 3:7-13**.   What were some of Adam and Eve's reactions to their disobedience?

16. In **Genesis 3:14-19**, God tells each of the three involved in this tragedy their consequences for disobeying his command.   Briefly describe those consequences as listed in Scripture.

   • **The Serpent**:

   • **The Woman**:

   • **Adam:**

17. After Adam and Eve were driven out of the Garden of Eden, Eve soon became pregnant. Read **Genesis 4:1** and explain how she responded to Cain's birth.

18. Read **Psalm 139:13-16.** How involved is God in the birth of a child?

19. From reading about Cain and Abel in chapter 4, we can easily see their different interests even though they had the same parents. Briefly describe how they were different.

   • **Cain**

   • **Abel**

Life Time

20. Please read **Genesis 4:2-7**. How did Abel's sacrifice differ from Cain's?

21. Reflect on the sacrifices of Cain and Abel. Which one required the most effort and explain why?

22. List some ways that we can teach our children the importance of following direction and obeying what we ask of them.

Own Time

23. How could Eve have been discontented in the Garden of Eden? Read **1Timothy 6:6-9.** How can discontent lead to deception? Examine areas of your life where discontent may be robbing you of godliness and leading you into temptation. Pray that the Lord will show you these areas and help you to pursue godliness with contentment.

24. Read **Romans 5:12-14** and **1 Corinthians 15:20-22.** Don't forget how the promise of Jesus' sacrifice relates to **Genesis 3:15.** God not only gives us hope, but he, in his infinite love, gave his first two children, Adam and Eve, hope when he cursed the serpent whom John in **Revelation 12:9** identifies both as Satan and the dragon. Praise God for crushing Satan's head.

"When the perishable has been clothed with the imperishable, and the mortal with immortality, then the saying that is written will come true: 'Death has been swallowed up in victory. Where, O death, is your victory? Where, O death, is your sting?' The sting of death is sin, and the power of sin is the law. But thanks be to God! He gives us the victory through our Lord Jesus Christ (1 Corinthians 15:53-57).

25. Now write out a prayer praising God for his Son, our ultimate redeemer.

~ The Creation ~

~ Author Unknown ~

When I created the heavens and the earth, I spoke them into being. When I created man I formed him and breathed life into his nostrils. But you, woman, I fashioned. I breathed the breath of life into man because your nostrils are too delicate. I allowed a deep sleep to come over him so I could patiently and perfectly fashion you. Man was put to sleep so that he could not interfere with the creativity of ME.

From one bone I fashioned you. I chose the bone that protects man's life. I chose the strong yet delicate rib which protects his heart and lungs and supports him, as you are meant to do. Your characteristics are as the rib, strength yet delicate and fragile. You provide protection for the most delicate organs in man, his heart and lungs. His heart is the center of his whole being, his lungs hold the breath of life. The rib cage will allow itself to be broken before it will allow damage to his heart and lungs. Support him as the rib cage supports the body.

Around this one bone I fashioned you. I shaped you. I created you perfect. Your eyes, don't change them, your lips how lovely when they part in prayer, your nose so perfect in form, your hands so gentle to touch. Oh yes, I've touched your hands, I've held your heart. Of all that lives and breathes you are the most like me. That is why I made you the mother of life. You see, you woman, reside in me.

Adam walked with me in the cool of the day and yet he was lonely. He could not see me, or touch me. He could only feel me. So everything I wanted Adam to share and experience with me I fashioned in you. My holiness, my strength, my purity, my love, and support, my protection. You are special because you are the extension of me.

Man represents my image, woman my emotions. Together you represent the totality of God. So man, treat woman well. Love her, respect her for she is fragile. In hurting her you hurt me. What you do to her, you do to me. In crushing her you only damage your own heart and lungs. Woman, support man as the rib cage. In humility show him the power of emotion I have given to you. In gentle quietness show your strength. In love show him that you are the rib that protects his inner self.

Next Time - Sarah

26. Read **Genesis 11:27-32**.   How is Sarai described in this passage?

27. Read **Genesis 12:10-20**. How is Sarai described in this narrative?

28. Briefly explained what happened in the above narrative.

Lesson 3 – *Sarah*

Real Time

Naming a child is a very important part of becoming a parent. When my husband Al and I were trying to decide on names for our firstborn in the spring of 1982, we had many an interesting discussion with many definite ideas about names. In fact, on our first date, our first small talk involved how we both hated our names—Joyce (could have been an elegant *Sherry* if there hadn't already been a Sherry Hasler in the family) and Alfred (named after a great-uncle he didn't know). Our middle names aren't much better. *Elaine* trailing *Joyce* soon became *Joyce Elainie* or *JoyciE.* Al's full name, *Alfred Louis*, wasn't exactly little league-friendly.

So when it came time to choose a name for our son, we knew it wasn't going to be an obscure one. The irony of choosing the common name of *Christopher* for him soon came back to haunt us. In his first grade classroom of 18 kids, with ten girls and eight boys, there were three *Christophers*—all of whom decided they wanted to be called *Chris*. So for years, really up until he was in high school, my only begotten son signed his Mother's Day card *Chris L* because that's what he learned in first grade.

The name we had chosen for our firstborn if female was *Cara Nicole*. I still love that name and will most definitely lobby for it if and when my children ever have their own children. But when faced with that decision two years after *Chris L* was born, I backed away from another *C* name. After all, I was already calling *Chris* the dog's name—*Scruffy*. The only similarity was that they both liked to eat, and there was a *C* near the front of each of their names. So Valerie Adele came into this world a little premature and a bit jaundiced but wearing a name meaning "strong and kind princess" even though when we first saw her she looked more like an oblong pumpkin than Cinderella. But now of course, we had an *Al* and *Val* in the family with both of their initials spelling their shortened names. But both soon got over it!

So when God renamed both Abram and Sarai, he certainly knew what he was doing. The name *Sarai* or as God preferred *Sarah* means "princess". He tells us why in **Genesis 17:15-16**:

God also said to Abraham, "As for Sarai your wife, you are no longer to call her *Sarai;* her name will be *Sarah*. I will bless her and will surely give you a son by her. I will bless her so that she will be the mother of nations; kings of peoples will come from her."

You see names are very important to God because as he speaks through the prophet Isaiah: "Can a mother forget the baby at her breast and have no compassion on the child she has borne? Though she may forget, I will not forget you! See, I have engraved you on the palms of my hands. . ." (49:15-16).

Our names are next to the nail scars on his hands. In fact, when I meet Jesus face-to-face for the very first time, I want to find my name there, stroke it gently, and then hold tightly onto his hand as we walk together.

Word Time

1. Read **Genesis 11:27-32**. How is Sarai described in this passage?

2. Now read **Genesis 12:10-20**. How is Sarai described in this narrative?

3. According to the notes from the NIV Study Bible, the Genesis Apocryphon (one of the Dead Sea Scrolls) praises Sarai's beauty who was 65 at the time this was written.

   What did Abram fear would happen if the Egyptians thought she was his wife?

4. Explain how Abram deceived the Egyptians.

5. How did the Lord treat the Egyptians after Sarai was taken into Pharoah's palace?

6. Fast forward to **Genesis 15:1-3**. Why was it so distressing to both Sarai and Abram that she had not yet conceived a son?

7. Continue reading verses **4-6** in **Genesis 15**. What did God promise Abram and how did Abram react? Why are both the promise and Abram's reaction significant?

8. Read **Romans 4:1-4**. How do works and faith interact?

9. Now read **Genesis 16**. How did Sarah's faith fall to her impatience here?

10. Read also **Hebrews 11:8-16**. Based on this passage, briefly explain how significant faith is in the life of a believer.

11. Thirteen years after Ishmael was born, God promised Abraham that Sarah would bear him the son of the covenant as promised in **Genesis 15**. Read **Genesis 17:15-22**, noting Abraham's reaction.

12. Really fast forward this time to **Genesis 21:1-7**. How did God keep his promise?

13. How old was Sarah when Isaac was born?

14. Isaac's name literally means "he laughs". How does that name fit as compared to how his parents reacted when they were told he would be born? See **Genesis 17:17** and **21:6.**

15. Isaac was a young adult when Abraham offered him up on the altar as described in **Genesis 22**. What new light does **Hebrews 11:17-19** shed on this event?

16. Read about Sarah's death in **Genesis 23:1-4**. She was 127 when she died. Briefly describe Abraham's reaction. What did this show about his love for her?

Life Time

17. Have you ever believed God's promises but grew impatient and then tried to make them happen in your timing with your own strength? Describe such a time in your life.

If you have, you're not alone. In **Genesis 16**, we see Sarai taking this offspring/inheritance promise into her own hands by setting Abram up with her maidservant Hagar. The jealousy between Hagar and Sarah birthed a sibling rivalry similar to the jealousy that Cain had toward Abel. But Hagar's and Sarah's rivalry generated a feud between nations that we still witness thousands of years later as the Middle East continues to erupt.

18. Describe how jealousy between family members can affect others years later.

19. Ishmael was 15 years older than Isaac, but both were greatly loved by their father Abraham. What kind of problems could have occurred between these two boys? What kinds of problems happen when siblings are spaced several years apart?

20. Later, in the New Testament, the apostle Paul sheds more light on the difference between Ishmael and Isaac. Read **Galatians 4:21-30** and explain what their mothers figuratively represent. How are we included in that description?

Own Time

21. Note any problems between your child/children or other family members that are caused by parental disagreements and/or jealousies. Ask the Lord to search your heart to see if any such friction exists in your family, and then pray, asking the Lord for insight, healing, and direction.

SARAH (copied from www.parenting.com)

Variations: SARA, SARAI, SARI, SARITA, SARKA, ZAHARIA

SARAH, SARA. Firmly in America's Top 5 — and approaching number one when you count both spellings — Sarah has been the premiere biblical girls' name here for two decades, offering rich Old Testament associations for those parents wishing to mine their religious roots and a sweet yet strong, patrician yet straightforward image to those in search of more secular name appeal. The big question: Are there too many Sarahs? While thousands of babies of all ethnic backgrounds throughout the country are given the name — the spelling ratio is generally three with the final *h* to every one without — Sarah has weathered trendiness perhaps better than any other contemporary female example. It's like one of the classic boys' names — Daniel, for instance, or David — in its ability to retain its widespread popularity without ever feeling dated. Long popular in England as well as here, in the Old Testament, Sarah was the wife of Abraham and mother of Isaac — who actually changed her name from SARAI at the age of ninety. Probably its most famous bearer, the great actress Sarah Bernhardt, was born Rosine. Two more contemporary actresses are Sarah Jessica Parker and *Roseanne*'s Sara Gilbert. Among the international variations on the theme are ZAHARIA (Greek), SARI (Hungarian), SARKA (Russian), and SARITA (Spain).

Next Time - Rebekah

22. Abraham, before he died, was still very concerned about God's promise and his own lineage. Read **Genesis 24:1-14** and briefly describe his plan for finding Isaac a suitable mate.

23. Rebekah's name literally means "at the well." Explain how that name is fitting.

24. How many sons did Rebekah and Isaac have, and what were their names?

Lesson 4 – *Rebekah*

Real Time

The very first woman at the well in the Bible was an answer to one man's prayer. Praying for our children's dates and mates is probably one of the most important things we do as mothers. Yet, I must confess that I don't do that enough. Thankfully someone, probably my grandmother, was praying for me to marry a Christ-loving man, and thankfully, God was listening.

Sometimes don't you wish you could just do as Abraham did? To commission your chief servant to go find your son or daughter a beautiful spouse from a desirable family lineage much like your own? Somehow in 21st century America, our kids, like we did, have much more freedom to choose their mates, a practice that leaves a lot of room for error and definitely the need for much prayer.

In thinking about this concept, I wanted a passage that we as mothers could pray for our children in their search for the right mate, hopefully a soul mate that loves the Lord. So I chose the one Paul prayed in Ephesians 3:14-19. I've added just a bit so that it fits the pre-marital mode:

"For this reason, I kneel before the Father, from whom his whole family in heaven and on earth derives its name. I pray that out of his glorious riches, he may strengthen you (*insert children's names*) with power (*to overcome sexual temptation*) through his Spirit (*choosing your spouse with godly discernment*) in your inner being, so that Christ may dwell in your hearts (*and the hearts of your spouses*) through faith.

And I pray that you (*insert children's names*), being rooted and established in love, may have power, together with all the saints, to grasp how wide and long and high and deep is the love of Christ, and to know this love (*and the love of a godly spouse*) that surpasses knowledge—that you may be filled to the measure of all the fullness of God."

I'm guilty of not praying enough for my children now that they are young adults. Another confession is that I still often just pray for their physical safety, especially when they're out late, driving alone. The story of Rebekah touches my soul because it really does illuminate how important prayer is for a parent. I think of Dr. James Dobson talking about his grandfather who prayed that his sons and their sons would all become ministers someday. When James decided to become a doctor, his family thought they had a black sheep. Yet look how Dr. Dobson has ministered not just to a local body of believers but to an entire nation and world. His grandfather's prayers were answered. So will ours be if we pray with the right heart, seeking God's will in both our own lives and that of our children. Remember God loves our children even more than we do.

Word Time

Abraham's chief servant, probably Eliezer of Damascus, was commissioned by a very worried patriarch to go find his son a suitable wife. Read **Genesis 24:1-5**; then answer the following questions:

1. In **verse 3**, what concerned Abraham?

2. Explain why Abraham would be bothered by this issue. Think back to God's covenant with Abraham.

3. What was Abraham's suggestion to his chief servant?

4. What concern did the servant have?

Note in **verses 12-14** that Abraham's servant prayed for success in finding a suitable mate for Isaac.

5. Specifically what sign did the servant request that would indicate the right mate for Isaac?

6. What would Rebekah's response to the servant's request for water indicate about her character?

Read **verses 15-21**.

7. How is Rebekah described in these verses?

8. How would her virginity connect with Abraham's concern for his lineage?

9. Read **verse 22** describing the gold nose ring and gold bracelets that the servant was to give Rebekah for agreeing to marry Isaac. What is significant about them and what does this indicate?

10. Review **Genesis 11:27-29**, and then read **Genesis 24:24**. How was Rebekah related to Abraham?

11. In **Genesis 24:48**, the servant clearly states how Rebekah is related to Abraham. But this verse also describes his response to God answering his prayer. What was that response?

Read **Genesis 24:50-58**.

12. How were Laban and Bethuel related to Rebekah?

13. What was their response to the servant's narrative as to how Rebekah was chosen?

14. What other gifts were given to Rebekah?

15. In **verses 54-58**, what did the servant want to do and how did Rebekah's family respond?

16. What does Rebekah's response in **verse 58** indicate about her personality?

17. If you will read **verses 62-67**, the story seems to end in what way? But that is not the end of the story. Read **Genesis 25:19-22**.

18. How old was Isaac when he married Rebekah?

19. What problem did they face in their marriage?

20. How did God solve the problem?

21. In **verse 23**, what prediction did the Lord make?

Read **verses 24-28**.

22. How many years had gone by in their marriage before Rebekah had given birth to the twin boys?

23. How could the above time period be significant? Think about how both Rebekah and Isaac might have parented the twins in lieu of this fact.

24. How were the boys different?

25. Why was Esau favored by Isaac?

26. Let's speculate for a minute. Why do you suppose Rebekah favored Jacob?

27. Read **verses 29-34**. What character weaknesses did each boy reveal?

28. Read **Genesis 26:7** and **Genesis 27:6-13** and **34-36**. What character flaw is seen in Isaac, Rebekah, and Jacob?

Life Time

29. What are some specific ways we as parents can avoid showing favoritism in how we treat our children?

30. Do you think birth order affects how you view your children? If so, please explain.

Own Time

31. Compare Abram's response in **Genesis 12:10-13** to Isaac's response in **Genesis 26:7**. What are the similarities of these responses?

32. Think about generational tendencies that have been passed through your family. Determine which ones are positive and which ones are negative, explaining why.

Next Time - Jochebed

33. Read **Exodus 1** and the first four verses of chapter 2. Briefly describe what was happening in Egypt at this time.

34. What motivated the midwives to let the baby boys live?

35. What did this Levite mother named Jochebed (**Exodus 6:20**) do with her newborn son?

Lesson 5 – *Jochebed*

Real Time

Today is literally the morning after—not from drinking too much or partying too late but from moving our youngest back to college to begin her junior year. We spent most of yesterday carrying boxes and bags up two flights of stairs in an unairconditioned dormitory that is almost as old as I am. This past week was preceded by almost two weeks of moving our son to Texas, same scenario but hotter with one more flight of stairs and a lot more stuff. So we've literally been on the move this past month with packing, checklists, and following each other down the road.

The day after both children are back in their own independent lives, no matter how hard I try, there is this emptiness that invades my heart. Along with missing their activity and having to share the bathroom and morning cereal, there's also a feeling of wanting to protect them and knowing full well that is impossible. With all the dangers of our ever-changing culture, I easily get trapped in ***worry mode*** concerning my children.

But our culture and my worries are nothing compared to what Jochebed faced when she was pregnant with her son Moses. Her people, the Israelites, were living as slaves in the foreign land of Egypt, where the king, or in their vocabulary, the ***Pharaoh***, issued a decree that all Israelite baby boys should be killed at birth. Jochebed showed amazing insight and faith as she found a clever way to not only protect her baby but to play a major part in his formative years. She balanced her need to protect him with an understanding that his future would necessitate giving him up and surrendering his future to God's will for his life. As we study Jochebed, note how when she trusted God to protect her child he gave him back to her. Trust is always a two-way connection.

Word Time

1. Please read **Exodus 1: 8 – 14**. How were the Israelites treated by their captors, the Egyptians?

2. Let's look at **Exodus 1:15- 17** together. Why would the king of Egypt, the Pharaoh, want the Israelite boys killed?

3. For just a moment, fast forward into the first book of the New Testament, the gospel of Matthew. In chapter 2, verses 13 – 18, a similar situation of danger for baby boys exists—this time reversed by location. What motivated Herod to want all Jewish boys two years old and under killed?

   • Hint: check out verses 1 – 6 of chapter 2.

4. According to **Exodus 1:16**, how did the Pharaoh propose that the baby boys be killed? What current cultural practice does this method resemble?

5. Looking back at **Exodus 1:17**, we find the reason the midwives let the baby boys live. What was that reason?

6. When Pharaoh questioned the midwives as to why they let the baby boys live, what was their response in verse 19? What that the truth?

7. Even though the midwives bent the truth, God was kind to them and gave them families of their own. According to verse 21, why were the midwives blessed?

8. The Pharaoh then issued a new order that demanded that all baby boys must be thrown in the river. Let's read together **Exodus 2: 1 – 4**. How did the Levite woman, identified later as Jochebed in **Exodus 6:20**, follow Pharaoh's order without killing her son?

9. How did Jochebed's above action reveal that she understood what Jesus explains in **Matthew 10:16-17**? What principle in verse 16 can we apply to parenting?

10. Let's continue to read in **Exodus chapter 2, verses 5 – 10**. What shrewd plan did Jochebed construct to protect her son?

11. Imagine with me for a minute what kinds of planning and observations had to happen for Jochebed's plan to work. Do you think she knew the routine of Pharaoh's daughter? If you answered "yes" or "maybe", how would Jochebed have known that if she had been hiding Moses?

12. How does Moses' sister (Miriam) well-timed question in verse 7 help save Moses' life? Do you think her presence there at that time was an accident? Why or why not?

13. What kind of trust would Jochebed had to have had in constructing the papyrus basket and leaving her three month old son in it along the bank of the Nile River?

14. Who did Jochebed put her trust in? How do you know?

15. How did Pharaoh's daughter's react to finding "one of the Hebrew babies"? What does this say about her character?

16. In order to save her son's life, what was Jochebed willing to risk?

17. How did God bless her for taking that risk? Please note all the blessings mentioned in verse 9 of Exodus 2.

18. Who named Moses, and what was the significance of his name?

19. Travel to the book of Hebrews in the New Testament and discover the great hall of faith chapter 11, finding verse 23. How did Amram and Jochebed respond to their son's birth of?

20. Why were Moses' parents not afraid of the king's edict?

21. In verses 24-28 in Hebrews 11, Moses' faith is further described. Pay attention to the reasons given for his faith. List those reasons below. Also note how the reason behind the faith affected Moses' actions and responses.

22. In less than five words, how would you describe Jochebed as a mother?

23. What attributes in Jochebed do you see in yourself?

24. As a mother, how would you like to be more like Jochebed?

Life Time

25. How did Jochebed's lifestyle and culture affect her role as a mother?

26. Briefly describe the culture we live in. How does it enhance and/or detract from parenting?

Own Time

27. Jochebed and her husband risked much to save Moses. Remember and record a few instances in your own life where you've taken risks on behalf of your children. Did these risks honor God?

28. In order to exercise faith, fear must be acknowledged and worked through. What are some fears that you have for your children?

29. Practically speaking, how can you exercise faith to overcome the fears listed above?

Next Time - Hannah

30. Read **1 Samuel, chapter 1**. How and why was Hannah suffering?

31. What does Samuel's name mean?

32. What did Hannah do to keep her promise after God answered her prayer?

Lesson 6 – *Hannah*

Real Time

Never mind that this is going to date me, but I grew up watching television shows like *The Brady Bunch, Leave it to Beaver,* and my personal favorite—*Please Don't Eat the Daisies.* The latter had an incredibly large family living in an old school with the plot focusing on the kids just running around the property. That sounded like my ideal for a family, but the show didn't last long. Guess the old-school, kids-running-wild motif couldn't obtain a renewal contract. It was reality TV three decades too soon.

Years later when my husband Al and I were trying to have our first child, I still envisioned a large family living in a home with lots of rooms with high ceilings and an outdoor paradise for them to explore. However, the reality became a quarter-acre lot in tract housing. Still there were lots of woods and open spaces around us. But what I didn't count on was that my body didn't do pregnancy well. So our first child was a miscarriage. Suddenly my dreams of a large family became a bit shaky. It was then that I ran to the Old Testament story of Hannah and Elkanah.

For those of you who have struggled with getting pregnant or staying pregnant, you understand the many emotions we go through after losing a baby. I felt defective somehow that I couldn't sustain what most women seem to do naturally. I can't imagine how Hannah felt when Elkanah's other wife, Peninnah, kept having children and taunting her.

Probably 1 Samuel 1:6 is one of the most upsetting understatements in the Bible for a woman wanting a child: "And because the Lord had closed her womb, her rival kept provoking her in order to irritate her." The King James Version puts it this way: "And her adversary also provoked her sore, for to make her fret, because the LORD had shut up her womb." The phrase p*rovoking her sore* certainly emphasizes Hannah's frustration. The Hebrew word for *provoke* (ka'ac) implies angering someone so much that they are raging with grief and indignation.

Needless to say, Hannah was angry, mad, and hurt. At Peninnah? Most definitely! At God? Probably! At her husband? Well, what do you think? Especially after he said two verses later: "Hannah, why are you weeping? Why are you downhearted? Don't I mean more to you than ten sons?" I can just hear her wailing get louder.

The range of emotions we feel after we've been hurt, provoked, and sometimes it seems, abandoned, often take us farther from God. Not so with Hannah! Her response to her barrenness is one worth studying, and one that we can apply in many other life circumstances. Now join me as we explore Hannah's desperation as she bathes it in fervent prayer.

Word Time

1. Let's read together **1 Samuel 1:1-2.** What do we learn about Elkanah's home life from this passage?

2. For both women, what type of emotional problems could arise from their marital situation?

3. Now let's travel farther into this family's home life by reading **verses 3 – 8**. What did Elkanah do year after year?

4. What does his obedience tell us about his worship of God?

5. How did he show favoritism between his two wives?

6. According to **verse 5**, what two reasons were given as to why Elkanah gave Hannah a double portion?

7. Year after year, how would that have made Penninah feel?

8. How could those feelings have caused her to provoke Hannah?

9. After reading **verses 9 – 11,** use one word to describe Hannah's state of mind? Explain why that word fits her emotions.

10. Think for a moment as to why Hannah would stand up to pray when most people bow down. Please write down your thoughts.

11. In **verse 11**, what three things did Hannah ask from God?

    1).

    2).

    3).

12. What did she promise as her part of the deal?

Now let's continue through **verses 12 – 17**.

13. Just as a reminder, let's review Eli's official position (see **verse 9**) and what could be some of the reasons he was watching Hannah so closely?

14. What was Eli's observation of Hannah as she prayed, and what was his conclusion?

15. How does Hannah explain herself and her actions to Eli?

16. In **verse 17**, what is Eli's response?

Life Time

Please read **1 Samuel 1:18-23**. After reading **verse 18**, I can't help but wonder if it was chocolate that she ate. For me, it would have been mint chocolate chip ice cream that would have made me feel better.

17. Note below what Samuel's name meant. How did you choose your children's names? Did they relate to any circumstances or people in your life at that time?

18. Note that Hannah spent time alone with her child when he was small. Do you spend quality time alone with each of your children? If not, how can you improve? Believe it or not, those years of chauffeuring kids around gave me many more opportunities to spend time alone with each of my children that disappeared when they both began driving. Use any time you can to listen to each child one-on-one.

19. Notice how much freedom Elkanah gave Hannah to mother Samuel as a young child (**verse 23**). How much freedom do you and your spouse give each other in parenting? How can this be improved?

Own Time

Read **verses 24-28** to complete the first chapter of **1 Samuel**.

20. Why did she present Samuel to Eli? (Reread **1 Samuel 1:11** as review.)

21. What principle(s) did Hannah teach her son by keeping that vow?

22. The first chapter of **1 Samuel** ends with Hannah stating that Samuel's whole life will be given over to the Lord. Please list some practical ways that we can encourage our children to give their whole lives to the Lord.

Next Week – Elizabeth

Please read **Luke 1:5-7.**

23. How is Elizabeth like Hannah?

24. Remember Abraham and Sarah. How was their situation and marriage similar to Zechariah's and Elizabeth's?

25. How are Zechariah and Elizabeth described?

Lesson 7– *Elizabeth*

Real Time

Have you ever known a woman that just by meeting her was an encouragement to you? I think Elizabeth, the wife of Zechariah and the mother of John, the Baptist, was such a woman. Her patience, her steadfastness, and wisdom just seemed to explode as seen in Luke, chapter 1. No wonder God chose her to birth his Son's forerunner.

One of the women that I know who fits this description is a member at my home church— Mount Pleasant Christian Church. Her name is Donna Clutts. Five minutes with Donna and the mandatory, accompanying hug refreshes my soul as much as reading my favorite psalm or eating a freshly baked chocolate chip cookie. (Oops, maybe the cookie isn't really a soul refresher but an appetite quencher!) She'll call and ask to pray for me. Of course, I pray for her, too. We have been doing much more of that now that her husband has had cancer.

It seems to me that Donna's way of encouraging springs from a genuine humility—that "inwrought grace of the soul"—that not only sees the Lord at work in everything but also sees the Lord at work in me. When she reminds me of how God is using me, I always feel a renewed sense of purpose and a refreshing strength. I know the Lord sends her with those hugs and those words at just the right time, just after or even during a self-inflicted *pity party.* I firmly believe all of us need a *Donna* or an *Elizabeth* in our lives to act as our God-ordained cheerleader. Without those encouragers and their encouragement, Satan has a stronger foothold in which to discourage or cause us to doubt God's purpose in fulfilling his will in our lives.

Imagine with me how much teenager Mary, the virgin mother of our Lord and Savior Jesus Christ, needed such an encourager. She had just been informed by Gabriel, an angel of God, the Most High, that she was carrying the Messiah, the Son of God. Even though that news was thrilling to her, she still had anxieties over being pregnant and wondering how the prophecy would happen. She also had to face the stares, the whispers, and the innuendoes from her kinsmen and from the townsfolk that being unwed and pregnant would generate. She needed a mentor and an encourager. She needed her cousin Elizabeth.

As we study Elizabeth, think about the people in your life who refresh your soul with their encouragement and their wisdom. Praise the Lord as you acknowledge how they come alongside you and lift you up just when you need it the most. Pray, too, how you can do that for others. Look for opportunities to share the simple blessing of a smile, a kind word, or a listening ear with someone who needs them. Believe me, lots of people need those simple blessings, myself included. Let's give as we have received, and abundantly more encouragement will flow through us and to us.

Word Time

Please read **Luke 1:5-7.**

1. What was Zechariah's occupation?

2. How was Elizabeth's ancestry similar to Zechariah's?

Before we go too much further, let's investigate what being a priest meant to the Jewish community. Moses' brother Aaron began the formalized lineage of Levite priests.

3. Read what God told Moses from the mountain in **Exodus 19:3-6**. God's intention for the people of Israel included two goals. What were those goals Moses was to speak to the Israelites?

4. Please allow a little digression here as we take a road trip to the book of Revelation where we see God's purpose for is people really comes full circle. Read **Revelation 5:10** and **Revelation 20:6**. What is God's plan for us in eternity? How does that relate to what the Lord revealed through Moses to the Israelites in Exodus?

Read Luke 1:8-17.

5. What was Zechariah doing when the angel of the Lord appeared to him? Read **Exodus 30: 6-8** for the original instruction as to this duty.

6. What was Zechariah's reaction to the angel's appearing?

7. What message did the angel convey?

8. What parenting instructions did the angel include with his message?

9. Many scholars think that Zechariah was instructed to raise his son as a Nazirite as described in **Numbers 6:1-4**. If so, he was a lifelong Nazirite, as were Samson (**Judges 13:4-7**) and Samuel (**1 Samuel 1:11**). Considering Zechariah's and Elizabeth's ancestry, how would this vow make sense? Also considering what John was to do, how would this instruction be fitting?

10. Zechariah was also instructed to name his son *John*, a Hebrew name that literally means "The Lord is gracious." Why is this name so appropriate?

Read Luke 1:18-25:

11. What question did Zechariah ask Gabriel?

12. What did this question convey about Zechariah's faith?

13. Speculate for a minute about why Gabriel left Zechariah speechless. Please write down some possible reasons why the angel took away his speech for awhile.

14. Elizabeth immediately became pregnant after Zechariah returned home. What does this imply about God's promises and his timing?

15. Referring to verse 25, describe Elizabeth's response to her pregnancy.

In Dee Brestin's book, ***The Friendships of Women***[1], she refers to missionary Dorothy Page's insight on the disgrace of barrenness:

"Until very recently, in most parts of the world, a woman has been seen mainly as a baby-producing machine, as someone to perpetuate the family line of the father …Even Martin Luther, great Christian that he was, stated, "If a woman becomes weary, or at last dies from child-bearing, that matters not; she is there to do it." For a woman not to become pregnant has usually been taken as a sign that she is displeasing to the gods and has been regarded as just grounds for divorce or the taking of a concubine."

---

[1] Brestin, Dee. *The Friendships of Women.* (Colorado Springs: David C. Cook, 2008), 198-199.

16. The name *Elizabeth* can mean either "worshiper of God" or "the fullness of God." How does each meaning apply to her?

17. Note some reasons why Elizabeth might have wanted to remain in seclusion for five months.

Read Luke 1:36, 39-45.

18. How far along was Elizabeth in her pregnancy when Mary visited her?

19. What was the baby's response to Mary's greeting to Elizabeth? How is this significant?

20. What was Elizabeth's response to Mary's visit? How does that show Elizabeth's humble encouragement to Mary?

21. In **verse 45**, what did Elizabeth specifically say about Mary's faith?

Life Time

Please read **Luke 1:57-66**.

22. **Verse 58** records that their neighbors and relatives shared her joy. How do we do that today in our culture?

23. How did these same neighbors and relatives react to the baby being named *John*? Why did that name surprise them? Is that tradition of naming a child after a family member still strong in your family?

24. Finally, how did they react to Zechariah's regained voice and his praising God? Explain why this same situation might or might not generate the same reaction in today's culture.

Own Time

25. Continue reading **Luke 1:67-80**. Now focus on **verse 80**. Where was John's strength? How did his parents nurture that strength? List ways that you nurture your children's strengths.

26. Reflect about all the people who have been encouragers to you. Choose one such person and write below how she (or he) has been there for you in times of need.

Next Time - Mary

27. In this lesson, we got a glimpse of Elizabeth's cousin Mary. Read **Luke 1:29-40** to get a clearer picture of her. How does Mary respond to the angel's announcement?

28. What impresses you about Mary from reading the above passage and explain why.

29. List some of the concerns or questions Mary might want to share with Elizabeth.

Lesson 8 – *Mary*

Real Time

Some people just seem to be born pure and innocent. Perhaps in our cynical cultural we call them *naïve*. But nevertheless, there is something refreshing about knowing someone who sees the world each day as if it were a new creation, a new adventure. I think Mary, the mother of Jesus, saw God and his creation each day with fresh, pure, and trusting eyes. I don't think Mary was perfect but she believed in a perfect will for her life by believing in a perfect Lord. No wonder she was chosen to mother God's "only begotten Son."

The irony is that she did not live up to her name's meaning because the name *Mary*, originally derived from the name *Miriam*, Moses' and Aaron's sister, means *"rebelliousness"*. Nowhere in the Bible does that definition fit Mary's character or personality. I wonder if the Lord was making a statement by having his Son be born of a woman whose name means and whose potential could be rebellion. What he might be saying to us is that by having Jesus a part of our lives, rebellion vanishes and purity surfaces.

Truly Mary, although not sinless, was a vessel willing to be used by God for his purposes and his will. Her final response to Gabriel, "Behold, the bondslave of the Lord; be it done to me according to your word" (Luke 1:38; NAS) illustrates her willingness to trust the Lord. The principle learned from Mary is not self-righteousness, but purity that comes from a willingness to be used by God no matter what.

Surely Mary had to face family that thought she had disgraced herself with a pre-marital pregnancy. Even Joseph, knowing that they had never had intimate relations, would probably wonder about her. But every Jewish girl's dream was to bear the Promised One, the Messiah. How would a young probably 15 year old girl shoulder that without rebellion?

The answer's pretty simple. She was willing to believe the Lord's Word and do his will. She only questioned how it would happen: "How can this be, since I am a virgin?" (Luke 1:34; NAS). She never questioned why. She never questioned God's choosing her. Her willingness to believe, to trust, and to rejoice in God's will made her "highly favored". Her purity and innocence came from her willingness to believe, trust and rejoice in her Lord.

Mary personifies one of my favorite verses in the Bible: "And without faith it is impossible to please God, because anyone who comes to him must believe that he exists and that he rewards those who earnestly seek him." I wonder if the writer of Hebrews 11:6 was thinking of the carpenter's fiancé when the Holy Spirit led him to write those words.

Word Time

Please read **Luke 1:26-40.**

1. After reading these verses, what impresses you
   about Mary?

2. Describe Mary's reactions to the news that she
   was to bear the Son of the Most High. What do
   these reactions show us about Mary's character?

Beth Moore, in her Bible study entitled *Jesus,
the One and Only*[1], states that **verse 39** reminds us
that "Mary got ready and hurried. . ." According to
Beth, "The words *got ready* offer us a delightful
possibility. The Greek word for this phrase is
anistemi, meaning 'to stand again; to cause to rise

---

[1] Moore, Beth. *Jesus, The One and Only*. (Nashville: Lifeway
Press, 2000), 19.

up.' Certainly the word could mean Mary simply rose up and departed. The wording could also imply that she got up off her face where she had fallen after the angel departed. The rest of the definition adds 'particularly spoken of those who are sitting or lying down; rising up from prayer.' If she didn't fall on her face, she was the exception to the rule in such visitations. Both Ezekiel and John the revelator had to be placed back on their feet! Mary may not have taken the news standing up either."

3. Think about and write down some of the concerns Mary might want to discuss with Elizabeth.

Now keep reading **Luke 1:45-56.**

4. Why does Elizabeth praise Mary?

5. **Verses 46-55** are called the Magnificat "because in the Latin Vulgate translation, the opening word is *Magnificat,* which means *'glorifies'.* (**NIV Study Bible** notes). How does Mary glorify the Lord in these verses? What are some of the specific things she praises about Him?

6. Now flash back to Hannah who offers up the same kind of praise to God in **1 Samuel 2:1-10**. What are some of the specific things Hannah praises the Lord for?

7. The incredible fact about Mary's prayer of praise in **Luke 1:46-55** is that she references 12 different Old Testament passages. What does

this suggest about Mary's knowledge of God's Word? What could be another explanation for her citing those passages?

Now read **Matthew 1:18-25.**

8. What was going through Joseph's mind after he found out the news of Mary's pregnancy? What guidance did the angel provide him?

Now read **Luke chapter 2, verses 1-7.**

9. What obstacles did both Mary and Joseph need to overcome as they became first-time parents?

10. How did Mary react when her son was born?

Continue reading **Luke 2:8-20**.

11. How did Mary react after the shepherds and angels visited them? Look carefully at **verse 19**.

12. The word used here as *treasured* is translated from the Greek verb *diatreo*, meaning *to store up*. It is also used later in the chapter as Mary and Joseph are anxiously trying to find Jesus after he's stayed behind at the temple. How does a mother *store up things in her heart* about her children?

13. Let's contemplate Mary's role as the mother of God's Son. During his lifetime, what personality traits of Jesus could have puzzled her?

14. Imagine how Jesus related to other children and his own siblings. How could he have been different? The same?

Life Time

If you are a mother, one of the most special things you can do for your children is to apply God's Word to their lives. One of the verses that I often tucked my son into bed with is found in God's reaction to his Son being baptized. Read **Matthew 3:16-17**.

15. How might a child react knowing his parents felt the same way toward him as God Almighty felt toward his Son?

16. What are some other ways we can affirm our children by using God's Word?

Own Time

One of my favorite ways to get my husband to go to weddings is to reference the passage from John 2 where Jesus attends the wedding at Cana. (And no, I don't tempt him with the idea of drinking wine.) Let's read **John 2:1-5**.

17. Let's dissect **verses 4** and **5.** What does Jesus question and how does Mary respond?

18. What does this dialogue between Jesus and his mother Mary reveal about their relationship?

19. How is their faith in each other revealed?

20. Think back to a recent conversation you've had with one of your children. How did that talk reveal your relationship with each other?

21. Here's a lottery-style assignment. List some ways that we can improve our relationships with each of our children. Be honest and practical.

Next Time - Salome

Soccer Moms, beware. You've met your match. Salome is petitioning the Ultimate Coach—Christ, the King. Read **Matthew 20:20-22**.

22. How did Salome approach Jesus?

23. From how she approached Jesus, how would you say she felt about him?

24. What favor did she ask of Jesus?

Lesson 9 – *Salome*

Real Time

Living in the shadow of the largest university in Indiana and attending high school in the late 60's influenced me to be socially sensitive. Sit-ins to protest the Vietnam War and flag/bra burnings (usually not simultaneously☺) were constant reminders that our nation was in turmoil. The cultural climate yearned for peace and a better, cleaner world. There was a definite sense that this world better not be all there is in life or the planet Earth was in major trouble. Southern Indiana even boasted of a few supposedly utopian communes where *hippies* and *flower children*, as those social protesters were media-nicknamed, came together to share everything.

So it's not surprising to me that Jesus' disciples felt much the same way about their culture. As Jews, they were living under Roman oppression with virtually no collective authority. The Jewish leaders didn't even have the authority to sentence Christ to death, using instead mob pressure to persuade the Roman ruler Pilate. Those closest to Jesus probably craved most fervently the new kingdom Jesus promised—the kingdom of God. They were just confused about its timing and its purpose. So in Matthew 20 when the mother of James and John approached Jesus, asking for special favors for her boys in this new kingdom, she expressed the hope of what many felt during this time.

Of all the mothers of the Bible we've studied, James' and John's mother Salome seems to be the most actively involved in her children's adult lives. She traveled with Jesus, constantly listening to his messages that predicted both hope and judgment. We can learn much from studying where she was during this time. John, the youngest disciple and the one whom Jesus loved very much, was probably her youngest child. Since some of the other mothers, even Jesus' own mother, had younger children still at home, they weren't as free to travel with Jesus as Salome was.

When I think back to how her fisherman husband Zebedee and she might have raised James and John, the one theory is that Salome must have been extremely outgoing and involved with her boys' friends. I'll even wager that she's the original Kool-Aid mom. Their home in Capernaum, the city that Jesus used as his home base for ministry, probably fed lots of hungry boys and later young men. I don't doubt that Jesus spent many a night there. Most likely lots of stories and laughter vibrated within their home.

Beginning with Eve and now ending with Salome, the past eight lessons have focused on mothers who never claimed to be perfect. They were simply women who struggled, like you and I do, to understand their roles and love and let go of their children when the time was right. With the exception of Jesus, none of these children were perfect either. But the Lord used their lives to further his perfect will in his perfect plan.

Word Time

Power, position and prestige—this triangle seems to be a major temptation the world continually throws at us. Today we're going to look at a mother and her two sons, who even after following Jesus, craved these three worldly *p*'s. But we're going to see how being with and continually following Jesus changed their priorities.

Please read **Matthew 20:20-22**.

1. Who approached Jesus in this passage?

2. How did she approach Jesus?

3. From how she approached Jesus, how would you say she regarded him?

Even in Bible times, a mother's identity was tied to being called so and so's mother, or in this case, the mother of her husband's sons. To have sons, as we learned when studying Hannah, was quite the blessing and one that many women envied. So this reference in Matthew was probably regarded as an honor, not a slight to Salome.

Let's back up a bit before going on to study her. We can learn a lot about a family by studying the children. Please read the following passages to learn more about Zebedee and his sons.

Matthew 4:21-22; Mark 19-20

4. What were the boys' names?

5. What were they doing when Jesus called them to follow him?

6. How sudden was their decision to follow Jesus?

7. What detail does the account in Mark give that Matthew leaves out?

8. How might the fact that Zebedee had extra help have made it possible for James and John to leave?

Now let's read Luke's account in **chapter 5, verses 1-11.**

9. How were James and John connected to Simon?

10. What did Jesus do that impressed his soon-to-be *fishers of men*?

11. How did that miracle make it easier for Zebedee and his wife to let their sons follow Jesus?

Now let's return back to James' and John's mother. Salome is only mentioned twice in the entire New Testament by name. Let's see where she is.

Please read **Mark 15:37-41** and **Mark 16:1**.

12. Where is Salome, and what has she just seen up close?

13. What had these women done for Jesus in Galilee? Specifically explain what that might have involved.

14. How do Salome's actions show us how she felt about Jesus?

Life Time

When we first met Salome, she was asking a special favor for her two sons that involved sitting on both sides of him while he was on the throne in the promised kingdom of God. Those positions next to a king indicated much power, authority, and prestige. Note how Jesus replied in **Matthew 20:22-23**.

15. Who did Jesus say had the authority to give away those positions?

16. What does his response tell us about his obedience to authority?

17. How can we apply his response to how we should react when we want position, prestige, power or authority?

18. What did Salome witness firsthand about Jesus doing his Father's will? (**Mark 15:37-41**) How might that have affected her? How does it affect us?

19. Finally how does the concept of sacrifice relate to following Jesus and being the kind of woman, the kind of mother, he has called us to be?

Own Time

Salome's youngest son John later wrote in **1 John 2:15-17** about three ways the world tempts us. Remember when we studied Eve that Satan tempted her with these three things the world offers us. Now we've just read about how John, along with his mother and brother, was especially tempted with the last one listed in **verse 16**.

20. Do you wrestle with any of those temptations? If so, which one seems to tempt you the most?

21. How does loving what's in the world take you away from following Jesus?

22. What's the promise for you found in **1 John 2:17**?

23. What are some ways you can do the will of God in your life?

Lesson 10 – *Real Love*

Real Time

As we close out our ten weeks of studying eight mothers of the Bible (*The Mob* as my husband calls them), my prayer is that we've learned much about ourselves from studying these everyday women. Also one of the real blessings in this study is always how much we learn from each other. Just knowing that we all struggle with the same problems is reassuring in itself.

Before the Holy Spirit directed me in this study, I had some *pie-in-the-sky, hunky-dory* notion that biblical families had it all together, never lacking in faith and focus, and the mother was always so perfect, so amazingly in tune with God. Well, a big relief came with the realization that these families had some real dysfunctional issues to deal with. Yet God blessed them by getting them through those times of sin and its consequences— from clothing naked Eve to setting a reward-motivated Salome straight.

As mothers, we often fight constant fatigue (laundry pile-up problems coupled with kids that don't sleep well at night) and continual worry (missed curfews and hateful "You can't tell me what to do!" looks). So we need each other. We need to know and lean on a God that is also a parent. I hold to the firm belief that we most understand God's heart and love for us when our own heart is concerned about our children. There's where our Lord and our Creator is most of the time in his relationship with us. So basically, when it comes down to it, as mothers, we get an up close, emotional glimpse into God's heart as to how much HE LOVES US!

JUST FOR FUN: Quick **Real Mothers** Review

Draw lines to match the descriptions with the **Real Mothers** from the Bible.

Eve   Her specialty: waterproofing baskets

Sarah   Her son really is perfect!

Rebekah   Pregnancy made her laugh.

Jochebed   Clothing style: Not a Problem!

Hannah   Likes her boys to finish first

Elizabeth   Sober while praying

Mary   The original woman at the well

Salome   Her husband was simply speechless.

Word Time

Salome's son John wrote five books in the New Testament—the gospel of John, 1, 2, 3 John, and the book of Revelation. Our last lesson is going to focus on many of his writings. He was also the youngest of the apostles and thought to have a very special place in Jesus' heart (**John 21:7, 20-24**).

1. **John 3:16** is the cornerstone of our Christian faith. Read this verse carefully, focusing on the words *gave* and *one and only son.* How does this statement show God's love for you and me?

2. Read what Jesus' own commentary on the meaning of that verse: **John 15:12-17**. What is the first command given in that passage?

3. In verse 13, how does Jesus describe what love is?

4. What are possible meanings behind this phrase, "to lay down his life for his friends"?

5. The Greek word for lay in verse 13 is *tithemi*, which also means "to bow, commit, conceive, give, kneel down beside." The image then is very much a loving posture, of coming alongside to take care of someone. How did Jesus do that for us on the cross?

6. How does Jesus continue "to lay down his life for us?"

7. Read **Romans 8:34.** Describe how Jesus is very active in your life right now.

Life Time

8. Jesus sacrificed and continues to sacrifice much for us. Think of a few ways that we sacrifice for our children and list them below:

9. In **John 15:14**, Jesus follows up his commentary about laying down his life by defining who his friends are: "You are my friends if you do what I command." From your study of these eight mothers of the Bible, what did you learn about how obedience is critical in a trusting relationship, like parent to child, friend to friend?

Own Time

10. Another commandment that Jesus gives us is also found in **John 15,** verse **17.** He simply says, "Love each other." Because that's a broad command, how do you balance loving your husband, children, and friends? To answer this question, decide who gets most of your time and energy. Are you happy with this balance?

11. We've also studied the importance of prayer in a mother's life. Please write each of your children's names below and one request that you want to pray daily on their behalf.

12. Now go back to thinking about yourself (for a change) and write down how you want to improve your relationship with each child. Write their names and how you would like the Lord to strengthen your relationship. Now pray that the Holy Spirit will show you ways how to make those relationships stronger.

Afterword

Thanks so much for being a part of this *Real Mothers* Bible Study. My prayer is that you'll enjoy being a mother who loves both her family and the Lord Jesus Christ with all your strength (We need it!), all your mind (What's left of it!), all your heart (Broken but still together. . .), and all your soul (Amen, Sisters!).

Your sister and fellow mother in Christ,

Joyce Long

www.ingramcontent.com/pod-product-compliance
Lightning Source LLC
Chambersburg PA
CBHW030013110426
42741CB00032B/482

* 9 7 8 0 9 8 1 6 9 8 3 4 2 *